Evaluating and Weeding Collections

in Small and Medium - sized Public Libraries

The CREW Method

by Joseph P. Segal

American Library Association   Chicago 1980

The preparation of this study was supported by the U.S. Office of
Education and the Texas State Library. The first printing in 1976 and
the second printing in 1979 were made by the Texas State Library under
the title of The CREW Manual.

The activity which is the subject of this report was supported in
whole or in part by the U.S. Office of Education, Department of Health,
Education and Welfare. However, the opinions expressed herein do not
necessarily reflect the position or policy of the U.S. Office of Education,
and no official endorsement by the U.S. Office of Education should be
inferred.

Although this work was originally published by the Texas State Library,
the opinions expressed herein do not necessarily reflect the official
policy of the agency.

ISBN 8389-0314-2
Printed in the United States of America

Contents

Acknowledgments

I wish to express special thanks to Linda Schexnaydre, Coordinator, Continuing Education, Texas State Library, for suggesting and encouraging this manual; William M. Duncan, System Coordinator, Library Systems Services, and Barbara Cockrell, Director of Lovett Memorial Library, Pampa, Texas, for on-the-job counsel and editorial advice; and Saida Yoder, Weatherford Public Library, Joyce Chestner, Boyce Ditto Public Library (Mineral Wells, Texas), and Cynthia Bennett, Lewisville Public Library, for practical advice and field testing the preliminary drafts. Appreciation also goes to Venus Hoggard and Carolyn Miller, Library Systems Services staff, Fort Worth Major Resource System, for typing the original manuscript for this manual.

Introduction

This manual is designed for use primarily by community and branch librarians who are the members of the profession shortest on time, space, and budget, but who are nonetheless as anxious as the directors of the largest city libraries to provide their patrons with efficient, effective service in a pleasant, attractive library environment. To achieve these ends, an entire range of indirect, "technical" services, such as selection, cataloging, and weeding must be carried out. However, the scarcity of staff and urgent demand for direct public services, such as reference and circulation, often prevent some of these indirect services being done adequately.

There is little in the professional literature that gives practical, clear, detailed advice on how to carry out the technical services. Library science courses are often more theoretical than practical. The harried community librarian is reluctant to devote her own precious time to devising effective ways of performing routines the value of which may not be very clear. This manual attempts to describe clearly, practically, and step-by-step, a new method of carrying out the five processes of "reverse selection": inventory, collection evaluation, collection maintenance, weeding, and discarding.

The Circle of Service: Where CREW Fits In

The method called CREW (Continuous Review, Evaluation, and Weeding) integrates all five processes into one smooth, streamlined, and on-going routine that assures that all these necessary indirect services are accomplished and accomplished in an effective way.

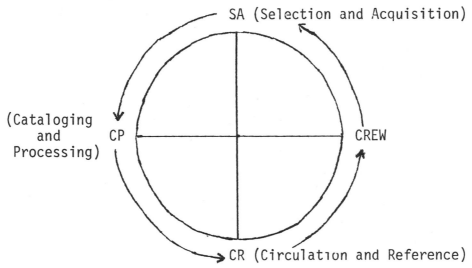

The above diagram represents the flow of library services direct and indirect; it is a circle because each process leads into the next. The whole cycle is called "collection building" - a series of on-going routines that continuously adds to, removes from, interprets, and adjusts the collection to fit its users and potential users.

> SA is the Selection (through reviews and requests) and the Acquisition (ordering and paying for) of the library's materials.

> CP is the Cataloging (including classification) and Processing (accessioning, stamping, pocket-pasting) of the same materials.

> CR is the step which includes the preparation of the books for the shelves and their use in Circulation and Reference, the public services.

Immediately after entering Circulation and Reference (CR) use, the library materials enter the CREW processes of inventory and maintenance. When, through evaluation and weeding, the librarian discovers that the material's useful career is over, it is retired by discarding. Meanwhile, CREW is generating information on the current strengths, weaknesses, gaps, and saturation points of the collection which the librarian uses in another round of Selection and Acquisition (SA). At each step, the librarian uses her special knowledge of library science and library materials and the particular community to meet the needs and demands of the library's users and potential users. CREW is a vital part of good library service. A library that does not evaluate, weed, or discard is like a cart wheel with a fourth of its rim missing. Too many community libraries today are having a rough ride on such a broken wheel.

Why Weed? Why CREW?

Why are these CREW functions so important, even necessary, for a good, useful community library? Haven't many community libraries done a good job for years without weeding? Isn't CREW simply a fancy name for throwing away books and slowing down a library's growth?

The Six Benefits of Weeding

There are six major benefits of weeding and especially of CREWing.

YOU SAVE SPACE. Discarded materials no longer cost money for cleaning, binding, mending, extra stacks, extra catalog drawers, and all the other hidden costs of maintenance which are not cut by lack of use. The librarian will not need to fill the bottom shelves or pile books on top of the stacks and the library will be more attractive and easier to use. There will be space to furnish tables and chairs for in-house study. And that open, friendly appearance that is the trademark of a good community library will be maintained.

YOU SAVE THE TIME of patrons, of the staff, and best of all, of yourself. Crowded shelves, full of ragged books with illegible markings, cost time for anyone looking for a particular book, for pages trying to shelve, or for the librarian trying to use the collection for reference. Filing and using the catalog are impeded by drawers full of worn cards. Library housekeeping, from dusting to relocating Dewey classes, is impeded and made more back-breaking by an overload of useless books.

YOU MAKE THE LIBRARY MORE APPEALING by replacing ragged and smudged books and unattractive rebounds with attractive new books. Circulation can be increased by simply making the shelves look nicer, even if there are fewer books.

YOU WILL ENHANCE YOUR COLLECTION'S REPUTATION for reliability and up-to-dateness and build public trust. It has been said that patrons feel that library books are selected by experts, and to some, the mere fact that a book is in the library, lends authority to it. A fifteen-year-old "pre-Mariner" book on the planets can give the library a credibility gap of astronomical dimensions.

The CREW method provides a CONTINUOUS CHECK on the need for mending or binding, alerts the librarian to lost or stolen books in need of replacement, and guarantees a more accurate volume count.

Finally, CREW provides CONSTANT FEEDBACK ON THE COLLECTION'S STRENGTHS AND WEAKNESSES. This information can be helpful in inviting donations. For example, knowing that the business books are out-of-date, the librarian can approach an organized group or an individual and request well-defined assistance in building an area of special interest and usefulness to them.

CREW keeps the present shape of the collection clearly in mind and helps in planning future directions for it. CREW integrates, not only its own five functions, but every function performed. CREW helps the librarian see the cohesion of every task performed in the library and to see the purpose of every task in relation to the patrons and the collection.

These advantages of weeding, and in particular of CREW, point out the truth of the old Chinese proverb: "Less is more."

The CREW Method in Ten Steps

The actual methodology of CREW is deliberately simple. The original pro-
cedures have been streamlined through field tests and careful discussion
of the actual situation of real community libraries. Top priority in a
community library is rightly given to direct service with a human touch.
To cut the time and effort required for indirect services, CREW has been
streamlined to ten steps, in four time groups, with allowance for stopping
this work to attend to patrons. The first step needs to be done only once;
the other nine steps form an on-going process which should be continued
for the duration of the collection.

One general question of method, frequently asked: Should weeding be done
by the head librarian only, or may it properly be delegated? Since the
situation varies greatly from library to library, a rule of thumb should
be never to let anyone weed who does not already take part in the selection
of new materials. On no account should the librarian delegate this function
to a volunteer who cannot view the library from the long-range perspective
the staff has developed through many regularly-scheduled hours working with
and thinking about the collection.

STEP ONE: MAKE WEEDING A PART OF POLICY. Obtain the Board's approval of
  a written weeding and discarding policy, as a defense against possible
  controversy, and as a guide in the day-to-day weeding. If a selection
  policy (a highly recommended item) already exists, the weeding policy
  could form an amendment or appendix to it. Check any legal restraints
  since some town charters contain rules about disposal of public property, including library materials. If a selection policy does not
  already exist, establish a definite gift policy allowing you to accept,
  decline, and dispose of gift books according to your discretion. The
  following are sample sections that can be added to the library's selection policy statement in the areas of weeding and gift books:

  WEEDING: "Materials which no longer meet the stated objectives of
  the library will be discarded according to accepted professional
  practices as described in the publication, The CREW Manual. Disposi-
  tion of library materials so weeded will be at the discretion of the
  librarian, subject to all relevant provisions of the Charter of the
  Town of _____, and the statutes of the State of Texas."

  DONATIONS: "Acceptance of gifts (of books and other library materials) will be determined by the librarian on the basis of their
  suitability to the library's purposes and needs in accordance with
  the library's stated acquisitions policy. Use or disposal of gift
  material will be determined by the librarian."

STEP TWO: BUILD WEEDING INTO THE YEAR'S WORK CALENDAR. Set priorities
  (those areas of the specific collection most in need of weeding should

6

be weeded first) and <u>schedule</u> the times when you will CREW the collection. As a rule of thumb, one CREWing of an entire collection should take approximately a year, although the first, most thorough, CREWing may well take longer. Allow plenty of time for the CREWing. If done in a careful manner, weeding is a slow process requiring thought and judgment. If there is a peak season for one sort of books (e.g., 500's just before the school science fair), schedule that section for a later time to make the inventory more accurate. Plan to do the weeding during slack hours and slow seasons when there will be minimal distractions.

STEP THREE: SHELF-READ the shelf about to be CREWed to insure proper order which, in turn, will make inventory much easier and more accurate.

STEP FOUR: GATHER EQUIPMENT on a book truck at the shelf intended for CREWing: 1) the appropriate drawer from the shelf list; 2) a sheaf of slips for the various disposal categories (either a mimeographed form, such as the one illustrated, or blank slips of paper); 3) a colored pencil for inventory (change the color each year so you can spot a book returned after inventory); 4) a note pad and pen; 5) a piece of cardboard; and 6) this manual for reference.

DISPOSAL SLIP

ANYWHERE PUBLIC LIBRARY

( ) Bindery

( ) Mend

( ) Consider for Replacement or New Edition

( ) Sell to Public

( ) Sell for Pulp

( ) Donate to _____

( ) Trade with _____

( ) Destroy

STEP FIVE: FOR WEEDING, study the shelves one book at a time, allowing stretches and coffee breaks to keep yourself alert. Do not do so much at one time that concentration and good judgment are lost. Use the Guidelines Tables beginning on page 10 of this manual, but also feel free to alter the formulas to fit your particular case, using your experience and knowledge of your community. Note any alterations in the margin of this manual (as with Sears and Dewey tables) to maintain local consistency. Place a slip in those books needing treatment or discard (marking the category of handling needed), and replace the books that are fine "as is." If you stop the work temporarily, mark the stopping point with the cardboard. When you stop for the day, turn the shelf list card for the last book considered on edge or tag that card, to mark the starting point for the next day. As a double check, note the call number of the last book on the pad. You may also wish to make notes as you proceed, for a later display, booklist, or locally prepared index (e.g., an index to short story anthologies).

STEP SIX: CHECK THE LIBRARY'S HOLDINGS. At the same time you weed, you will take inventory. When examining a book for weeding, make a check mark with the colored pencil on the verso of its title page and on the shelf list card for that book next to the accession number for that copy. Do not check books that are not physically on hand, unless your circulation system is one of the few that file in Dewey order (in which case the books on loan, but not overdue, can be checked in the classes you are doing). In all other cases, take all books returned to the desk after their classes are CREWed without this year's inventory check on their title-page versos, and mark their versos and their shelf list cards prior to placing them on the open shelf. Over a year's time, this method will show you which books are, in fact, lost, stolen, or strayed, and which should be considered for replacement. Any book still unchecked on the shelf list six months after its class is inventoried, may safely be presumed to fall into this category, unless you know it to be at the bindery or long overdue and in process of being retrieved.

STEP SEVEN: CHECK THE PULLED BOOKS AGAINST THE INDEXES the library holds. This process will alert you to a possible high reference-usage item, since the indexes will continually be directing patrons and staff to this book. Such a case might suggest special exemption from the general rules of weeding, and if the book is physically worn, a need for non-circulating status. (See the Bibliography, page 23 for a list of standard library indexes.)

STEP EIGHT: TREAT THE PULLED BOOKS ACCORDING TO THEIR SLIPS.

1) Bindery: Prepare bindery forms for books needing binding and store them for the periodic bindery pick-up.
2) Mending: Do the required mending or put the books aside for a clerk or volunteer to mend.
3) Discard: Process the discards by removing all ownership marks; pulling the shelf list and catalog cards for last copies, or crossing out the accession number on the shelf list for duplicates; tearing off the book pockets and book cards; and putting the discards on the book-sale table, storing them for an annual sale, or recycling, or boxing them for burning, garbage pick-up, or the pulp dealer. If recycling, place all cards into the book pocket. The recipient library will have a head start placing the book in circulation if cards accompany the book.
4) Replacement: Place aside for careful consideration, each book needing replacement by a new copy, new edition, or better title on the same subject.
For types of disposal, see page 17 of this manual.

STEP NINE: REPLACEMENT CHECKING AND ORDERING. Make replacements at the
    conclusion of weeding a major Dewey Classification. Compare the
    weeded books with titles in recent editions of selective biblio-
    graphies for possible replacement titles. Further, if the library's
    collection does not contain any recommended titles in a specific
    area, consider ordering these listed titles (unless they are in
    little demand). Selective bibliographies might include the follow-
    ing (additional titles are on page 23):

> The Children's Catalog (Wilson)
> Public Library Catalog (Wilson)
> Fiction Catalog (Wilson)
> Books for Public Libraries: Selected Titles for
>   Small Libraries and New Branches (Bowker)
> Reference Books for Small and Medium-Sized Libraries (ALA)
> Science and Technology: Purchase Guide for Branch
>   and Public Libraries (Carnegie Library, Pittsburgh)

It might also be helpful to consult lists of award-winning books
such as Pulitzer Prize Books, National Book Awards, Best Books for
Young Adults (ALA), Notable Books (ALA), as well as, bibliographies
in Library Journal and those prepared by the Regional Public Library
Systems and Major Resource Centers in Texas. Check reviews of new
books for the last year and Books in Print for replacement or sup-
plementary titles or new editions.

Place a gold star on the book pocket of each book slated for replacement before re-shelving it, and mark "TBR" (To Be Replaced) in soft
black pencil on the author and shelf list cards. (This step will
alert you to pull the book and possibly to pull or revise its cards
when the replacement comes in). Prepare the orders for the replacements, with the note, "Repl. (call number)," on the bottom of the
order slip as a signal to pull the older book when the new copy is
received.

STEP TEN: SET UP DISPLAYS for low-circulation, high quality books that
    would benefit from better exposure. Plan the displays to be color-
    ful and relevant to current community concerns. If the book still
    does not circulate, consider it a candidate for trade with another
    library or for "recycling."

If done routinely every day, this review of the collection will expand
your knowledge of the library's holdings, give you a reservoir of possible
reference sources, and prepare you for informed selection of new books on
the basis of actual usage and the actual strengths and weaknesses of the
collection. You may possibly want to coordinate selection of new science
books to coincide with CREWing of the 500's. In this way, the feedback
between the present collection, its use, and future directions will be
strong and direct. This subject-grouping of selection also facilitates
allocating purchases evenly to each area of major demand, as opposed to
an unplanned way of casually scanning issues of Library Journal and Booklist.

The CREW Guidelines for Weeding Your Collection

The formulas given here for the various Dewey classes are rules of thumb based on professional opinions in the literature and practical experience. The formula in each case consists of three parts: 1) The first figure refers to the years since the book's latest copyright date (age of material in the book); 2) the second figure refers to the maximum permissible time without usage (in terms of years since its last recorded circulation); 3) the third refers to the presence of various negative factors, called MUSTY factors. For example, the formula "8/3/MUSTY" could be read: "Consider a book in this class for discard when its latest copyright is more than eight (8) years ago; and/or, when its last circulation was more than three (3) years ago; and/or, when it possesses one or more of the MUSTY factors." Most formulas include a "3" in the usage category and a MUSTY in the negative factors category. The figure in the age category varies considerably from subject to subject. If any one of the three factors is not applicable to a specific subject, the category is filled with an "X".

MUSTY is an easily remembered acronym for five negative factors which frequently ruin a book's usefulness and mark it for weeding.

> M = Misleading (and/or factually inaccurate)
>
> U = Ugly (worn and beyond mending or rebinding)
>
> S = Superseded (by a truly new edition or by a much better book on the subject)
>
> T = Trivial (of no discernible literary or scientific merit)
>
> Y = Your collection has no use for this book (irrelevant to the needs and interests of your community)

On the following pages are the CREW Guidelines by Dewey Class. On page 21 is an Overview Chart of the CREW Formula.

CREW Guidelines by Dewey Class

000 (General)

020 (Library Science)   10/3/MUSTY

030 (Encyclopedias)   5/X/MUSTY   *Stagger replacement sets (e.g., replace Britannica in 1976, World Book in 1978, Americana in 1980, then a new Britannica in 1982); one new encyclopedia at least every ten years.*

other 000's   5/X/MUSTY

100 (Philosophy and Psychology)

150 (Psychology)   10/3/MUSTY   *Try to keep abreast of popular topics.*

other 100's (Philosophy)   10/3/MUSTY   *Value determined mainly by use.*

200 (Religion and Mythology)

Try to have something up-to-date on each religion represented by a church, synagogue, or other assembly in your community.   10/3/MUSTY

or

5/3/MUSTY   *Use 10/3/MUSTY except for areas of rapid change such as Roman Catholic and Episcopal liturgy and doctrine which are 5/3/MUSTY.*

300 (Social Sciences)

See that controversial issues are represented from all views and that information is current, accurate, and fair.

310 (Almanacs, Year-books)   2/X/MUSTY   *Seldom of much use after two years; add one, discard one every year, to keep only last three years in the collection. All public libraries in Texas should have at least one general almanac and the Texas Almanac; need only last decennial census.*

320 (Political Science)   5/3/MUSTY   *For topical books; historical materials are judged more on the basis of use: 10/3/MUSTY.*

340 (Law)	10/X/MUSTY	
350 (Government)	10/X/MUSTY	*Or repeal or constitutional reform, whichever comes first.*

370 (Education)	10/3/MUSTY	*Keep historical materials only if used. Discard all outdated theories; check with a teacher or principal if in doubt.*

390 (Etiquette, Customs)

Etiquette	5/3/MUSTY	*Keep only basic, up-to-date titles.*
Folklore, Customs	10/3/MUSTY	

400 (Linguistics and Languages)

	10/3/MUSTY	*Discard old-fashioned and un-appealing textbooks and school grammars. Need only stock dictionaries for languages being studied or spoken in your community.*

500 (Pure Sciences)

510 (Mathematics)	10/3/MUSTY	
570 (General Biology and Natural History)	10/3/MUSTY	
580 (Botany)	10/3/MUSTY	
other 500's	5/3/MUSTY	*But keep basic works of significant historical or literary value, such as Darwin's Origin of Species, or Farraday's Chemical History of a Candle.*

600 (Applied Sciences)

610 (Medicine)	5/3/MUSTY	*Except Anatomy and Physiology which change very little: X/3/MUSTY*
630 (Agriculture)	5/3/MUSTY	*Keep up-to-date; be sure to collect information on newest techniques and hybrids, if you serve farmers or ranchers, Keep Yearbook of Agriculture for last ten years, earlier if in demand.*

640 (Home Economics)	5/3/MUSTY	*Be strict with old sewing and grooming books in which styles change rapidly; however, keep cookbooks unless very little used.*
690 (Manufactures)	10/3/MUSTY	*Keep books on old clocks, guns, and toys since these items are often collected.*
other 600's	5/3/MUSTY	*Technology is making such rapid advances that any material over five years old is to be viewed with suspicion. One major exception: repair manuals for older cars and applicances should be kept as long as such items are generally kept in your community.*

700 (Arts and Recreations)

745 (Crafts)	X/3/MUSTY	*Retain basic technique books if well illustrated.*
770 (Photography)	5/3/MUSTY	*Check closely for outdated techniques and especially outdated equipment; if in doubt, check with local photography club or buffs.*
other 700's	X/X/MUSTY	*Keep all basic materials, especially histories of art and music, until worn and unattractive.*

800 (Literature)

	X/X/MUSTY	*Keep basic materials, especially criticism of classic writers. Discard minor writers no longer read in the local schools, unless there is an established demand among non-students.*

900 (History and Geography)

910 (Travel and Geography)	5/3/MUSTY	*For guidebooks such as the Fodor series and for descriptive or scientific geography.*

	10/3/MUSTY	*For personal narratives of travel, unless of high literary or historical value.*
other 900's	15/3/MUSTY	*Main factors: demand, accuracy of facts, and fairness of interpretation. Discard personal narratives and war memoirs of World War II, the Korean War, and Indochina War, in favor of broader histories of these conflicts, unless the author is a local person, or the book is cited in a bibliography as outstanding in style or insight. Discard dated viewpoints, e.g., the McCarthy Era "World Communist Conspiracy" theory of modern history. Retain all Revolutionary War materials until the Bicentennial ends in 1983, since many papers will be required on the subject.*
<u>B (Biography)</u>	X/<u>3</u>/MUSTY	*Unless the person treated is of permanent interest or importance, such as a U.S. President, discard a biography as soon as demand lessens. This rule especially applies to ghost-written biographies of faddish celebrities. Poor quality biographies of major figures should be replaced with better ones, if funds permit. Biographies of outstanding literary value, such as Boswell's <u>Life of Johnson,</u> are to be kept until worn, without regard for the biographee's reputation.*
<u>F (Fiction)</u>	X/<u>2</u>/MUSTY	*Discard works no longer popular, especially second and third copies or old bestsellers. If a book deposit or branch are planned, you might store these for such a purpose. Retain works of durable demand and/or high literary merit; a good, non-topical, well-written novel appealing to universal concerns will continue to circulate at a moderate rate for many years.*

YA, J, and E Fiction   X/3/MUSTY   *Discard children's and young
                                                   adult fiction if the format
                                                   and reading level are not ap-
                                                   propriate to the current in-
                                                   terest level of the book.
                                                   Discard topical fiction on
                                                   dated subjects; discard
                                                   abridged or simplified clas-
                                                   sics in favor of the original;
                                                   discard as many series books,
                                                   particularly second and third
                                                   copies, as possible.*

J and E Non-Fiction

*Use adult criteria, but
look especially for in-
accuracy and triviality
which are common faults of
over-simplified children's
non-fiction.*

Periodicals
    (Including Newspapers)   3/X/X   *Bind only those periodicals in
                                                   constant use for research and
                                                   listed in Reader's Guide and
                                                   other indexes in your library.
                                                   If financially feasible, buy
                                                   microfilms of heavy-demand
                                                   magazines. For the local news-
                                                   paper, see section, "Local
                                                   History." Clip other periodi-
                                                   cals and newspapers sparingly
                                                   for the vertical file before
                                                   discarding.*

Vertical File and Government Documents

    VF   1/2/MUSTY   *Weed the vertical file rigor-
                                                   ously at least once a year.
                                                   Keep only materials on topics
                                                   of current interest on which
                                                   no books yet exist. Often a
                                                   book will be published on a
                                                   subject within six months after
                                                   the material is placed in the
                                                   vertical file. Date all mate-
                                                   rials when added to the file.*

    College Catalogs   2/X/MUSTY   *Keep current; keep only those
                                                   catalogs from colleges of in-
                                                   terest to students in your area
                                                   and one or two universities of
                                                   national importance.*

Audiovisual Materials	WORST	Worn out, Out of date, Rarely used, System headquarters can supply, or Trivial and faddish. Since many media are costly, weeding of such materials, once acquired, must be done as carefully and cautiously as the initial selection and acquisition.
Local History	X/X/X	Your library is also the logical archives of the community, and in many cases, of the county. Retain all books on the history and geography of the city and county; all local newspapers (on microfilm if possible); all accounts of travels through your immediate area; all memoirs of local figures; and all local city directories. Keep most books by local authors (if of any literary value); and some genealogies of important local families. Collect local photographs, playbills, and other ephemera of possible interest to future writers in your area. If possible, start an oral history program; the tapes thus produced, being unique, are not subject to the WORST criteria. If local history materials, particularly unique or rare items, begin to wear or become soiled, make them non-circulating.

What To Do With Weeded Books: Types of Disposal

The CREW method is well suited to the simple, pre-printed disposal slip (placed in each book when it is pulled) which indicates whether the book is to be sold, recycled, or destroyed; or mended, rebound, or replaced. Mending should be done as soon as possible to forestall further damage. Mending should not require longer than fifteen minutes nor be so extensive as to ruin the book's appearance. Rather than being mended, the book should be sold and replaced (if use warrants) with a newer copy or edition.

There are basically only four ways to dispose of a book:

DESTROY IT: by burning in an incinerator or by tossing it into the trash.

SELL IT: to the public, either at a large annual sale or from a continuous exhibit; or to a used-book dealer or pulp dealer, usually in large lots.

RECYCLE IT: donate book to a hospital, charitable institution, Indian reservation, poor school district, or to a small non-system library struggling toward system membership.

TRADE IT: with another library, or with a used-book dealer, for a book your library can use.

Each method of disposal has its advantages and drawbacks, and, its own pre-conditions.

DESTRUCTION should be reserved for the worst books, the absolutely hopeless cases, and only if the books cannot be sold for pulp. The advantage of this method is that it requires minimal time and effort. The major drawback is that it derives no benefits, in money or public relations, from the discarded books. This method of disposal is also the likeliest to cause a "weeding controversy," since many people are shocked by the "waste" of throwing "good books" on the trash heap. Also, "book burning" has unpleasant connotations. If you can explain that only the worst of the weeded books get this treatment, you will avert unpleasant publicity.

SELLING promotes good public relations and is potentially mildly profitable if you sell books of some residual value and with the clear understanding that the books may contain dated information. Those books which you cannot sell should be destroyed or sold, with other hopeless cases, to a pulp dealer (if one is within driving distance). Make clear the firm policy, explained to each buyer via a sign, never to accept your own discards as donations. Mark all discards clearly to avoid donations from well-intentioned, but ill-informed, patrons.

RECYCLING is not a profitable method, but promotes even better public relations, if only very good discards are disposed of in this way. Giving away junk does not promote good public relations, nor does it help the recipients. A day-care center, for example, will remember your donation of some picture books even if the covers are shabby. You may gain a regular customer for your prettier new picture books and a dozen regular patrons for your preschool story hour by sincerely considering the wants and needs of the recipient of your discards.

TRADING your "best" discards is both excellent public relations and a shrewd financial move. Trading works only with two specific classes of discard: the high-quality (or, at least, well-reviewed) book that is nonetheless of no interest to your community (e.g., a shelf-sitter in Del Rio might be dynamite in Pampa, and vice versa); or the occasional donated duplicate of a good book of less than two-copy demand. Inquiries about trades can be made over the phone, by letter, or as part of the festivities at the Texas Library Association Annual Conference or system meetings.

Before sending a book to a bindery, compare the cost of rebinding with the cost of a new copy or edition. A rebound book is simply not as attractive as a new book. In some cases, however, notably out-of-print titles, rebinding is the best option. However, often a new copy is almost as inexpensive and is more appealing. Possibly, you might want to remove and save the plastic covered dust jacket from the book before sending it to the bindery since it might fit the rebound volume.

Encouraging the Hesitant Weeder – An Epilogue

Hopefully this manual has already shown the place of weeding in the cycle of library service, the benefits of regular CREWing, and the streamlined simplicity of the CREW method. However, there are five often heard objections to rigorous weeding. Since they serve to justify keeping collections unweeded and unreviewed, they need to be considered in this manual.

I AM PROUD OF HAVING A LARGE SELECTION OF BOOKS TO OFFER MY PATRONS. BESIDES, I NEED TO HAVE ENOUGH VOLUMES IN THE COLLECTION TO REMAIN A SYSTEM MEMBER.

BUT - Quality counts more than quantity, both with the patrons and with the Texas State Library. Annual statistics that show virtually no discards, while they will not disqualify you for system membership, could indicate that the collection may be growing outmoded and haphazard. A good library is not necessarily a big library. The level and quality of service the library can offer is of utmost importance. Of course, while the collection is still very near the minimum required, you simply cannot weed quite as strictly as a library safely over the requirement. However, once the volume count exceeds 12,000 (or 27,000), full-scale CREWing should be done in earnest. For service, efficiency counts more than raw size.

IF I THROW THIS BOOK OUT, I JUST KNOW SOMEONE WILL ASK FOR IT TOMORROW.

BUT - This situation seldom actually occurs and is certainly less common than a patron asking for a book not acquired by the library. The "weeded needed" will be few, are less harmful to public relations than a habitually cluttered and unreliable collection, and can be accessed through the Texas State Library Communications Network. Moreover, CREW cuts the "asked-for unacquired," by alerting the librarian to gaps, losses, and the full range of materials available.

WELL, THIS OLD BOOK MAY BE RARE AND VALUABLE, EVEN A FIRST EDITION!

BUT - Even if the old book dates back before 1900, chances are one in several thousand that an it is worth as much as $25.00. Only a handful of unique copies, authors' personal copies, or other treasures sell for more than this amount. Old books are overwhelmingly rubbish or cheap curios. They almost never deserve the glass-fronted cases or separate stacks they too often receive at the expense of library space, time, money, and usefulness. "First Editions" are also worth very little except in rare cases where only a handful of copies remain. The first edition of an unimportant book is worthless, even if it is unique. A high-priced ($30.00 or more) First Edition is almost always a classic or near-classic which was not appreciated when first published. If you have never heard of the title, it almost certainly is not of this sort. If you still think you have a valuable book, send a detailed description of it (more than on the catalog card and including a physical description with condition and any printer's marks) to a reputable antiquarian book dealer for his estimated auction value of the book. (Most real rare books are sold at auctions in New York or London.) Otherwise, take the possibly rare book to the Major Resource Center Library to check the description against American Book Prices Current which lists books auctioned during the past year and the price each brought.

IF I DISCARD A BOOK BECAUSE IT HAS NOT BEEN USED, ISN'T THAT ADMIT-TING PUBLICLY THAT I MADE A MISTAKE IN SELECTING IT?

SO? Every librarian makes those kinds of mistakes. Selection is not based on scientific formulas or objective measurements. To a very large extent, selection has to be based on the librarian's judgment of books and people. Judgment can be sharpened by train-ing and experience, but it can never be made infallible.

ISN'T WEEDING REALLY JUST IRRESPONSIBLE DESTRUCTION OF PUBLIC PROPERTY?

NO. As explained in the first part of the manual, weeding is a very constructive process which increases the library's ability to give a "full service value per dollar" and which improves the appearance and comfort of the library building. As for "irresponsibility," the CREW method's very first step involves checking any possible legal constraints specifically to avoid violating civic responsibilities. Further, destruction by trashing or burning, is not the only method of disposal; in fact, it is the last-choice option.

WE NEED TO HAVE SOMETHING ON THIS SUBJECT. AND WE NEED EVERY COPY OF THIS CLASSIC FOR THE SCHOOL RUSH.

BUT - Consider the options: Those extra copies could be kept in a storage room until the rush or replaced with clean, easy-to-store, attractive, inexpensive paperbacks. If "something" is needed on a subject, then something good that will be used is needed. If it will not be used, a book, even the only book on a subject like paleo-botany, is simply cluttering the shelves. If an unused book clutters an inaccurate book is worse. If you really need something, acquire something new, accurate, well-written, and sturdily bound.

The point of weeding, and of CREWing, and of all other library functions, technical or public, is to provide your patrons better service, clearer access to the world's knowledge, and entertainment. By streamlining your collection for efficient and reliable use, you are making it easier and faster for the people of your community to find the facts, phrases, and stories they need. Therefore, take this manual and discuss the matter with your Board. Think about it for a while. Then, start working toward efficient, effective service and a high quality collection: Start weeding this year.

Overview Chart of CREW Formulas

<u>Dewey Class</u>

<u>000</u>	020	10/3/MUSTY
	030	5/X/MUSTY
	Others	5/X/MUSTY
<u>100</u>	150	10/3/MUSTY
	Others	10/<u>3</u>/MUSTY
<u>200</u>		10/3/MUSTY
<u>300</u>	310	2/X/MUSTY
	320	5/3/MUSTY (Topical)
		10/3/MUSTY (Historical)
	340	10/X̄/MUSTY
	350	10/X/MUSTY
	370	10/3/MUSTY
	390	5/3/MUSTY (Etiquette)
		10/3̄/MUSTY (Folklore and Customs)
<u>400</u>		10/3/<u>MUSTY</u>
<u>500</u>	510	10/3/MUSTY
	570	10/3/MUSTY
	580	10/3/MUSTY
	Others	5/3/MUSTY
<u>600</u>	690	10/3/MUSTY
	Others	5/3/MUSTY
<u>700</u>	745	X/3/MUSTY
	770	<u>5</u>/3/MUSTY
	Others	X̄/X/MUSTY
<u>800</u>		X/X/MUSTY
<u>900</u>	910	5/3/MUSTY (Geography and Guide Books)
		10/3/MUSTY (Narratives)
	Others	15/3/MUSTY
<u>B</u> (Biography)		X/<u>3</u>/MUSTY
<u>F</u> (Fiction)		X/<u>2</u>/MUSTY
<u>YA, J & E Fiction</u>		X/3/MUSTY

J & E Non-Fiction	Adult Criteria; Stress <u>M</u> & <u>T</u>
Periodicals	3/X/X
VF (Vertical File)	1/2/MUSTY
College Catalogs	<u>2</u>/X/MUSTY
AV (Audiovisuals)	WORST (See page 16)
Local History	X/X/X

Bibliography

Standard Selective Bibliographies

*American Library Association. Reference Books for Small and Medium-Sized Public Libraries. Chicago: American Library Association, 1969.

Baker, Augusta. The Black Experience in Children's Books. New York: New York Public Library, 1971.

*Books for Public Libraries: Nonfiction for Small Collection. 2nd ed. New York: Bowker, 1975.

Cheney, Frances Neel. Fundamental Reference Sources. Chicago: American Library Association, 1971.

Courtney, Winifred (ed.). Reader's Adviser. 11th ed. New York: Bowker, 1968.

Dobie, J. Frank. Guide to Life and Literature of the Southwest. Revised. Dallas: Southern Methodist University, 1952.

Useful for older Texans; a guide to what to keep in older Texas collections.

Eakin, Mary K. Good Books for Children. 3rd ed. Chicago: University of Chicago, 1966.

Jordan, Lois B. Mexican Americans: Resources to Build Cultural Understanding. Littleton, Colorado: Libraries Unlimited, 1973.

Library Committee. National Association of Independent Schools. 4000 Books for Secondary School Libraries. 3rd ed. New York: Bowker, 1968.

Wilson Standard Catalog Series:

*Children's Catalog. 12th ed. Bronx, New York: H.W. Wilson, 1972.

Senior High School Library Catalog. 10th ed. Bronx, New York: H.W. Wilson, 1972.

*Public Library Catalog. 6th ed. Bronx, New York: H.W. Wilson, 1973.

Junior High School Library Catalog. 2nd ed. Bronx, New York: H.W. Wilson, 1970.

*Fiction Catalog. 8th ed. Bronx, New York: H.W. Wilson, 1970.

<u>Indexes</u> *(Consider keeping books which are indexed in these standard works.)*

Brewton, John E. and Sara W. (eds). <u>Index to Children's Poetry</u>. Bronx, New York: H. W. Wilson, 1942. (Supplements: 1957, 1965)

Cook, Dorothy E. and Isabel S. Monro. <u>Short Story Index</u>. Bronx, New York: H. W. Wilson, 1953. (Supplements: 1950-1973)

Dickinson, A. T., Jr. <u>American Historical Fiction</u>. 3rd ed. Metuchen, New Jersey: Scarecrow Press, 1971.

Not highly selective, but useful for determining books to be kept.

Fidell, Estelle A. (ed.). <u>Play Index</u>. Bronx, New York: H. W. Wilson, 1953-1973. (Four volumes)

Hagen, Ordean A. <u>Who Done It?</u> New York: Bowker, 1969.

A selective list and index to mystery and suspense fiction, including short story collections and some juvenile novels.

Smith, William James. <u>Granger's Index to Poetry</u>. 6th ed. New York: Columbia University Press, 1973.

<u>Further Readings</u>

Carter, Mary D., et al. <u>Building Library Collections</u>. 4th ed. Metuchen, New Jersey: Scarecrow Press, 1974. Pages 163-176.

Sinclair, Dorothy. <u>Administration of the Small Public Library</u>. Chicago: American Library Association, 1965. 2nd ed., 1979.

Slote, Stanley J. <u>Weeding Library Collections</u>. Littleton, Colorado: Libraries Unlimited, 1975.

<u>Booklets and Pamphlets</u>

<u>Reasons for Weeding</u> (Technical Leaflet #30). Austin, Texas: Texas State Library, 1969.

<u>Sample Policy Statement for Public Libraries in Texas</u>. Austin, Texas: Texas State Library, 1969.

<u>Weeding the Children's Book Collection</u> (Technical Leaflet #53). Austin, Texas: Texas State Library, 1971.

<u>Weeding the Small Library Collection</u> (Small Libraries Project Pamphlet #5, Supplement A, Revised edition). Chicago: American Library Association, 1972.

Periodical Articles

Allen, William H. "Call the Junkman Last," <u>Catholic Library World</u>, v. 36 (April, 1965), pages 497-9.

How to dispose of weeded books.

Coppinger, Joyce. "Recipe for a Successful Book Sale," <u>Mountain-Plains Library Quarterly</u>, v. 16 (i.e., 17, Fall, 1972), pages 13-14.

Erlick, Martin. "Pruning the Groves of Libraro," <u>Wilson Library Bulletin</u>, v. 50 (September, 1975), pages 55-58.

Lists thirty "criteria for <u>not</u> discarding books from a public library."

*Rush, Betsy. "Weeding vs. Censorship: Treading a Fine Line," <u>Library Journal</u>, v. 99 (November 15, 1974), pages 3032-3.

*Schurter, Jo. "Re-cycling Discards," <u>Library Journal</u>, v. 97 (September 15, 1972), pages 2911-12.

Strain, E. W. "Weeding Without Pain," <u>Oklahoma Librarian</u>, v. 24 (July, 1974), pages 22-23.

Book fair for systems librarians.

"Weeding the Collection," <u>Unabashed Librarian</u>, v. 16 (Summer, 1975), pages 7-12.

Wezeman, Frederick. "Psychological Barriers to Weeding," <u>ALA Bulletin</u>, v. 52 (September, 1958), pages 637-9.

Periodicals

<u>The De-Acquisitions Librarian</u>. The Haworth Press, 174 Fifth Avenue, New York, New York, 10010. Quarterly; $16.00/year; index.

A new periodical created to help librarians in the development, management, and evaluation of an on-going weeding program in their libraries and to provide a great variety of weeding methods and approaches. The purpose of the periodical is to "discuss the problems involved in the creation and maintenance of secondary storage areas; cooperative programs related to weeding; rational collection development and limited library growth; the relegation of weeded stock; and the relationship between weeding, use studies, and improved acquisitions." The first issue (Spring, 1976) includes an article entitled, "Weeding Monographs in the Harrison Public Library," and a good rational on the importance of weeding.

Many of the titles listed in this bibliography are available on loan from the Professional Librarianship Collection, Texas State Library, Box 12927 Capitol Station, Austin, Texas 78711.

*Highly recommended.